MW00881196

GET
IN THE
Sales
GAME!

GET IN THE GAME! Sales

The Playbook for Winning in Sales When the Game Has Changed

Written by

SUSAN "SWEET SUE" KOUCHIS

Your Author Journey Begins Here

Quantity Purchases:
Companies, professional groups, clubs, and other organizations may qualify for special terms when ordering quantities of this title.
For information, email info@ebooks2go.net, or call (847) 598-1150 ext. 4141.
www.ebooks2go.net

Published in the United States by eBooks2go, Inc. 1827 Walden Office Square, Suite 260, Schaumburg, IL 60173

ISBN: 978-1-5457-5432-0 (Paperback)
ISBN: 978-1-5457-5427-6 (Hardcover)

Library of Congress Cataloging in Publication

CONTENTS

INTRODUCTION

March 2020 was a pivotal moment of new change in the world of sales. With many countries and states shut down by stay-at-home orders, our normal way of sales life was rocked to its very core. Sales professionals who use face-to-face, handshake, ground game, and give-a-hug styles of selling had to power pivot to stay in the game.

Three words come to mind: *fear*, *anxiety*, and *stress*.

This book talks about those three words and how this could impact our success in the selling process.

Energy, family, health, wealth, sex, teeth, faith, and gratitude are also mentioned in this book. Health is wealth, and energy is power! Think of the last time you showed gratitude or did a kind act for someone! How did you feel? Did you feel amazing? That is the energy and passion you need to create long-lasting customers. Money will always come when you give gratitude and come from a place of energy and passion.

I wrote this book to help sales professionals learn new techniques and strategies to get them to the top of their game. I'll show you how to reach the C-suite faster and easier than ever before. You'll also learn to reach new prospects and close new business to win success.

I hope this book helps sales professionals with tips and tricks in selling in the *new* world of sales. Grit and hustle will never go away. But in this new era of sales, passion, marketing, and energy will be the keys to survival.

THIS IS MY STORY

My name is Sue Kouchis, but many people just call me Sweet Sue. They call me this because they say I'm someone who is *sweet*, has amazing energy, and loves life. I find it rather flattering!

I decided to write this book to share my sales story of how I became successful during a pandemic. I want to share it with the world, and I hope that by doing so I can help others to become better sales professionals, even during a global crisis.

Many of you reading this will probably ask, "What makes Sue qualified to write this sales book? Is she making millions of dollars?" Well, you will never know! A true sales professional never brags about the money they make. You're in control of being healthy and wealthy. This book will get you started on an amazing path to health, wealth, and success.

I started in sales thirty-five years ago. It was a time when companies just gave you your business cards, a phone and said, "There's the door. Go sell."

Some of you will know what I'm talking about. I started my career in radio sales. Tough job when starting out, but great experience. I was at a Logistics company for twenty-five years in sales and held many job titles: local sales, global sales, national sales, sales manager, and sales director. Looking back, I'm amazed I stayed and survived with one company for twenty-five years. I changed jobs and have been with my present company, RIM Logistics, for five years.

Behind every great sales professional is a *great team*. The team behind you can make or break you. Just recently, one of my customers had a critical airfreight shipment coming from Germany to the United States. This was so critical that if it were not delivered on a Sunday, this would impact their year-end numbers. As the old saying goes, everything that could go wrong did. There were Covid issues, airline outages, and driver delays. Our team was all hands on deck, and operations monitored this shipment all day Saturday and into the night. I even went to church and lit a candle to pray to the freight gods. At 1:00 p.m. on Sunday, our team delivered the freight. I tell this story because I was so impressed with our operations and management team.

They weathered every storm, but hung on and got the job done. This gives me confidence that our company is the *best* at what we do. You must have absolute confidence that your company or product is the best.

When I started at my new company, I started with zero revenue. Starting from zero revenue is never a warm and fuzzy feeling. But when you have a great team behind you, anything is possible. I must report, since Covid, I've had the best year of my entire career, and I am just *getting started*.

Before 2018, fear, anxiety, and stress had crippled me in my selling process. Fear kept me from chasing the big deals. In my mind, I would tell myself, "I'm not good enough," or "I'm not smart enough." I'm sure some of you reading this book know what I'm talking about. Well, everything changed for me in 2018 and also in this past year of Covid. These changes in my journey have brought me to where I am today.

This pandemic has given me a new way of selling and has made me rich with energy and passion. Since the pandemic,

I've had explosive growth in my career. I've made many power pivots I want to share.

Yes, I'm afraid some people will judge me for writing this book or think it's not very good. I went back and forth many times on whether I should write and publish it or not. Finally, I said to myself, "Hell yes! Let's do this!"

I want to share new tricks and golden nuggets of wisdom with the world, especially in this new world of selling. I'm not a writer—just a fifty-nine-year-old sales professional, a wife, and a mother who wants to help others. This book is raw, real, and from the heart.

I'd like to say a big thank-you to my loving family for their help in my journey. I couldn't have done this without your unconditional love and support.

Now let's get to it!

CHAPTER ONE: GET FIT

How many sales seminars or books mention fitness and say that having a healthy mind and body can lead to being successful? Not many. Many sales books talk about "killer closes and the best close techniques," or having the best IBS (Initial Benefit Statement) as well as many other buzzwords and processes.

But they don't talk about what's *real*. Anxiety, fear, and stress are the *real* killers in life and in the sales process. We need to destroy these emotions with pure freaking energy (PFE)!

Moving the body and being hydrated are very important in maintaining high energy levels. Energy is power and the golden ticket to success. With a healthy mind and a quick hit of pure energy, stress, anxiety, and fear will diminish. Customers are looking for people who have good energy and who can tell a great story with passion. No one wants to work with Mickey the Mope—that is, someone with no energy!

Let's face it: our traditional style of selling has changed. So how do you get that burst of energy? Here's a hint: move your body. A quick set of ten push-ups, ten sit-ups, and ten leg crunches can get your energy levels up!

Even standing up and moving your arms quickly in a runner's stance will get that energy flowing.

Check out Brian Bradley's content. Brian has many exercises for great bursts of energy as well as sitting and standing exercises: @thebrianbradley.

Did you know starting your morning with a cold shower increases blood flow, reduces anxiety and stress, and is great for the immune system? Another great benefit of cold showers is healthy hair and glowing skin. Plus, it's free.

FEAR, FEAR, FEAR

Fear is found among all humans. I recently read an Instagram post from Sara Blakely, founder of Spanx: "The two things people are most afraid of [are] fear of failure and fear of being embarrassed," she said in an Instagram post she uploaded in October 2020. "I'm constantly working on both of these fears, so I can live the life I want, free from the burden of caring [about] what other people think of me."

Overcoming these fears is "required to pursue your dreams," she continues. For her, it takes practice.

Oftentimes Blakely will intentionally do things to embarrass herself "so that the fear of embarrassment loses its power over" her.

Reduce fear using a smile! Did you know putting on a great smile when you're ready to call a customer or preparing a personal video can get your energy up? Try it! Also, standing in a superhero pose can help with creating positive energy and reducing fear and anxiety.

Experts at Harvard University state that positions like this decrease the stress hormone cortisol. Cortisol levels can decrease by up to 25 percent, testosterone can increase by up to 20 percent, and risk tolerance can increase by up to 33 percent.

Also, an excerpt from Harvard Health Publishing and Harvard Medical School, posted on March 28, 2016 says:

"Regular exercise such as cycling or gym-based aerobic, resistance, flexibility, and balance exercises can also reduce depressive symptoms. Exercise can be as effective as medication and psychotherapies. Regular exercise may boost [the] mood by increasing a brain protein called BDNF that helps nerve fibers grow.

"What is BDNF: Brain-derived neurotrophic factor, or abrineurin, is a protein that, in humans, is encoded by the BDNF gene. BDNF is a member of the neurotrophin family of growth factors, which are related to the canonical nerve growth factor. Neurotrophic factors are found in the brain and the periphery."

So health is wealth in sales! Why don't sales seminars talk about this?

Being consistent with your health will pay off big time. Check out my "Coronamama" workout video on YouTube. https://www.youtube.com/watch?v=Wdcp31uXHl0&t=19s Search for "Susan Kouchis coronamama" if you can't access the link. I have been doing this under-two-minute workout for years. It gives me a morning burst of energy and is a great start to my day. Even if your workout is minimal, don't worry—you will still see results.

Being consistent with your approach will give you the momentum you need to build a healthy mind and body. Remember that health equals wealth. Sales start with a healthy mind and body.

With that in mind, let's dive in deeper! Positive thoughts are important to maintaining a healthy mind.

An excerpt posted by the Mayo Clinic staff says: "Is your glass half-empty or half-full? How you answer this age-old question about positive thinking may reflect your outlook on life, your attitude toward yourself, and whether you're optimistic or pessimistic—and it may even affect your health.

"Indeed, some studies show that personality traits such as optimism and pessimism can affect many areas of your health and well-being. The positive thinking that usually comes with optimism is a key part of effective stress management. And effective stress management is associated with many health benefits."

Keep thinking positive thoughts and fueling your body with water. This will crush any curveballs thrown at you. You know what I am talking about. We've all been there. This will never change; however, with positive energy, I can say bring it on!

TEETH AND ORAL HEALTH

One of the secrets to sales success is teeth. Yes, I'm not kidding.

Make that dentist appointment and be consistent with your cleanings. Healthy teeth build confidence, which will help bring home many sales victories. Health is wealth, and it starts with being hydrated, moving your body, and maintaining healthy teeth.

I did some research and found that when a dentist looks in your mouth, they get a glimpse of your overall health. They can often see indicators of diabetes, heart disease, dementia, oral cancer, anemia, stress, and eating disorders.

If you don't believe me, here are the responses of some of the top dentists on how teeth cleanings can be an easy ticket to good health and energy: "When I examine a patient's mouth, there are a number of things that I am checking. With the help of x-rays, I obviously check for cavities, but I am also evaluating their mouth for gum disease. People with gum disease are more prone to heart disease, oral cancer, diabetes, stroke, respiratory infections, and dementia.

"Over half of pregnant women will develop a condition called pregnancy gingivitis. This condition causes bleeding, swelling, and redness or tenderness in the gums, and if any woman suffers from those symptoms, they should see their dentist more often.

"If I notice that something does not look right, I will refer a patient to their physician in order to address the problem early before more serious symptoms have time to develop. This way a dentist can alert a patient to an underlying problem that they may not be aware of. Thus, a proper cleaning and good home care are critical to good overall health and your general wellbeing" (Dr. Andrew J. Sampalis, DDS and Associates).

"Health is so much more than being free of disease. It encompasses mental health, spiritual health, and financial health. As a dentist, I attend to an intimate, sensitive, and visible organ of physical health: the mouth! Happy mouths free of disease lead to happy people."

"A mouth is so much more than simply 'teeth and gums!' The physical elements of the mouth assist with their chief physiological function: to eat and speak. But a mouth also produces smiles!"

"A dentist is a 'smile keeper!' Mother Theresa believed that 'peace begins with a smile.' The song goes, 'When you're smiling the whole word smiles with you.' Can a smile do all that?"

"What does a healthy smile and mouth tell people about us?

"Recent studies suggest that tooth loss is related to perceptions of success, job position and financial success. We lead with our smiles. They welcome people. They disarm and attract people. They help show kindness and empathy and understanding to others. Smiles give us confidence and help us feel good about ourselves."

"Think of visiting your dentist regularly for your checkup as another type of healthy spa treatment! Lay back and relax.

Take care of the health of your teeth for a lifetime of beautiful smiles that are more than just teeth" (Dr. Patricia Stifter, DDS, Palos Park, Illinois)!

So the lesson here: Don't skip the dentist. Schedule your appointment for success!

Yearly health checkups are important as well. Don't skip those yearly health checkups! They're very important to our positive energy. Early prevention is important in maintaining a healthy and positive life.

CLEANSES

Some people ask me, "How do you get your energy up, besides moving your body and staying hydrated?" Another great piece advice is doing a cleanse. There are many cleanse treatments. I started with the Whole 30 program by Melissa Hartwig. You can also check out the celery juice cleanse *Celery Juice* by Anthony William.

There are many programs to choose from, and consulting your doctor on the best cleanse is a good start for your health.

I started my cleanse program in January 2018, and it was a game changer. My energy level was at an all-time high, my anxiety, stress, and fear had diminished, and I dropped a few pounds. This gave me the momentum I needed to crush my goals.

I remember participating in a sales seminar in that same month, with all my colleagues across the world. In a roundtable forum in which we discussed our strategies for having a successful 2018, they called on me. I told them about my cleanse and how energy is power. I talked about giving back and about having gratitude. I'm sure most people wondered how that could possibly have helped me with my strategy.

Let me tell you how! With my newfound energy, my fear, anxiety, and stress all decreased. Giving back to my church with my time, talent, and resources made me feel overjoyed. I was having fun in my job again, my bedroom life was exciting, and I loved spending my time with my family. Yes, all these things are game changers to life and business success.

SEXUAL HEALTH

Here is another energy tip: sex. And not many talk about sex. So let's talk about sex!

Did you know that loving sex is a great way to bring your energy to a "peak state"? What is a peak state, you may be asking.

"The difference between peak performance and poor performance is not intelligence or ability; most often it's the state that your mind and body is in" (Tony Robbins).

The first component of the Tony Robbins triad is your physiology. Physiology refers to your body and all its systems, and by extension, elements that directly impact those systems. Physiology dictates our feelings, how we use our body, and affects how you feel mentally and emotionally.

If you want to master your feelings, you must be aware of how your feelings and your body are interconnected. If you stand up straight, you'll feel prouder and more alert. If you slump over and neglect your body, you're more likely to feel negative. The next time you find yourself in a bad mood, stand up and breathe deeply. You have the power to reset your mind and mood. Check out Tony's work if you want to read more about this concept.

Anthony Robbins's physiology concept also includes taking care of yourself. You know intuitively that you feel your best when you get enough sleep and nourish your body with quality food and nutrients. Even though it can be tempting to skimp on these things, don't take any shortcuts. Give yourself enough sleep to keep your mind clear and take the time to eat foods that make you feel full, nurtured, and healthy.

But back to the matter at hand—sex. Sex is not only pleasurable but also good for your health. Experts say that your sex drive can stay high even in your senior years. But all too often we lose energy as we age, and this affects every aspect of our lives from the boardroom to the bedroom.

"Never think that a lack of energy means an end to your sex life, and [that] there is nothing you can do about it," says Dr. Sharon Bober, director of the Harvard-affiliated Dana-Farber Sexual Health Program. "In fact, having sex can actually boost your energy levels as well as other aspects of [your] well-being."

Benefits include:

Better sleep: According to the AARP, sex helps us sleep more soundly because arousal and orgasm release oxytocin, also called the "cuddle hormone," and reduce the levels of the stress hormone cortisol.

A more youthful appearance: Couples who have sex three times a week appear ten years younger, according to research done by David Weeks, a neuropsychologist at Scotland's Royal Edinburgh Hospital.

A reduced risk of prostate cancer: According to Harvard Health, several studies have found that a high ejaculation frequency was linked to a 31 percent decrease in the risk of prostate cancer.

Fewer headaches: German researchers found that having regular sex reduced the frequency of migraines, according to the AARP, with 60 percent of the participants saying it reduced or halted their pain.

Stronger relationships: A 2014 study showed that even after forty years of marriage, couples who were sexually active were happier and more content in their marriages. The authors noted that sex doesn't have to mean sexual intercourse, but rather the physical contact between two people.

So have fun in the bedroom and get the energy going for great wins in sales! When that curveball comes, and you're in peak state, you will have the amazing ability to take a negative and turn it into a positive. In turn, this will create lasting success.

CHAPTER TWO: THE GAME CHANGER

The year 2018 was a game changer in my life. I was fifty-seven years old. My daughter, Karissa, came home one day and told me that Tony Robbins would be in Chicago for a three-and-a-half-day seminar called UPW (Unleash the Power Within). I had been a Tony Robbins fan for thirty-two years, since my company had sent me to a one-day seminar to see him in Milwaukee, Wisconsin. His passion and mission gave me strong fundamentals in the sales process, which gave me the momentum to jump start my career.

I was intrigued to go. I walked on fire at that seminar—yes, actual fire—and the rest of the seminar was also life changing. *Fear* I would say is a key blocker to holding us back from chasing our big dreams. I have to say, I was reluctant to walk on that fire, every emotion came over me.

To have the courage, mindset, and determination to walk on fire led me to one word: *unstoppable*. Energy was flowing in my body, and I was unstoppable. Tony Robbins's "peak state" helps you break through fear, anxiety, and stress. A small shift in your mindset can make a world of difference.

In the seminar, Tony talked about *fear* and not letting this emotion cripple you from contacting the C-suite. He challenged everyone that day to make ten contacts to C-level prospects. After walking on fire, becoming unstoppable, I was charged and *ready* for this challenge.

Tony Robbins has many companies, and one of his companies presented at the seminar. This company is called OsteoStrong, and the CEO, Kyle Zagrodzky, spoke at the seminar. OsteoStrong manufactures strength-conditioning equipment to help bone growth and people with osteoporosis.

I was intrigued in two ways. In my mind, this would be the first CEO I would contact and have no *fear* while doing it. Also, I have osteoporosis and thought I needed more information on how this could help with my bone growth.

OSTEOSTRONG team

So, after he got off the stage, I ran around the United Center looking for him. After twenty minutes of chasing him down, there he was. Ten people were waiting in line to talk to him about his product. I remember having no fear, but I thought, "What am going to say to Kyle to make him think I'm credible in a one-minute conversation?"

Let me set the scene. There were another fifteen people behind me waiting to talk to him. I said to myself, "Sue, you got this. No fear! Let's go." I went up to Kyle, with amazing energy, shook his hand and said, "Tony said we should reach out to ten CEOs. Kyle, you're my first CEO. My name is Sue Kouchis, director of sales for RIM Logistics. RIM is a full-service logistics company, and I want to help you deliver your product all over the world. Also, we have warehousing and distribution in the United States."

There was a pause. Then, he said, "Great to meet you, Sue. We could probably use your services."

Well, as you can imagine, I almost fell over! I gave him my card, and he asked me to contact him via LinkedIn. I took a picture of his badge so I had his spelling right. Well, after a year of meetings and negotiations, I'm pleased to report our company is doing business with OsteoStrong, a Tony Robbins company. That was the beginning of my new top-down strategy. People use LinkedIn for job opportunities. I use LinkedIn to find targets and prospects. We'll talk more about this in chapter 5.

UPW changed my life. At fifty-seven years old, I was the number-one salesperson in my company. This award afforded me the opportunity to see London, England, and experience Wimbledon—another thing I could check off my bucket list.

WHAT IS UNLEASH THE POWER WITHIN?

Unleash the Power Within is a live three-and-a-half-day event with Tony Robbins designed to help you unlock and unleash the forces inside that can help you break through any limit and create the life you desire. There, you can learn how you can surpass your own limitations to achieve your goals, improve the quality of your life, and build lasting greatness.

All you need is within you now. You can connect with the people, the passion, and the environment that will make it happen. One weekend can change everything.

And I'm not the only one who has benefitted from the UPW coaching. My whole family has benefitted.

After my daughter, Karissa, and my sons, Steve and Mike, attended UPW, life was never the same for my family. Karissa ended up working for TR as a speaker and host. Thank you, Karissa, for spreading your energy and passion to the world.

Steve was a sales engineer. He was unfulfilled in his job and decided to venture out on his own and started his own advertising company.

My other son, Mike, pursued his dreams of starting a high-end car wrap company from scratch. He is doing very well, even in these challenging times.

My husband, Pete, also went to Tony's training courses, UPW, and Business Mastery. Tony Robbins's Business Mastery seminar covers topics such as business strategy, business innovation, marketing, sales, and more so that you can grow a successful business.

With his newfound energy, his business survived the pandemic, and our relationship has flourished. I will talk more about his power pivot in business and his business success in chapter 4.

Chapter Three: Get In the Game and Power Pivot

We've been living in uncertain times in the world of sales during the pandemic. Few books, if any, have been written on sales success in a pandemic, so now is the time to write your own sales playbook.

Marketing through social media is the best way to connect with your customers. We need to market ourselves, and now more than ever. Video, video, and video are the keys to success! Personal videos sent through email, or posted on LinkedIn, YouTube, Instagram, Facebook, and other platforms have been out there for years. Many successful millionaires and billionaires have used these platforms to expand their reach and connect with their customers. A small percentage of salespeople use social media to expand, grow, and connect. So be creative. You're writing your own playbook for success!

Check out these great tips on marketing from these amazing women.

@AngieLeeShow: "Authentic always wins. It doesn't matter what you're selling-we all are craving GENUINE connection"

@alynauta, founder of connective consulting: "Despite the negative connotation around the word, we are all influencers at our core. Our ability to impact comes from purpose and our purpose is a combination of what we know + how we want to serve the world. When we lean into who we are over what we do, we become indispensable and abundantly fulfilled."

The sales professional who pivots, is creative, and is comfortable being uncomfortable will have much success. Use marketing to your advantage—be authentic, be passionate, be you. No nonsense initial benefit statements (IBS) or elevator pitches. Create your personal video story with passion!

We, as sales professionals, are in the digital economy of connecting with customers. Pivoting is essential to our success, especially now. Trying new concepts and strategies will bring home victories. Fear, stress, and anxiety are killers when it comes to public speaking and being behind a camera. Keep practicing, keep it simple and bring value by connecting with a great story. Let's face it: no one is perfect. It's okay to have a few stumbles. Be authentic, people want to connect with your personal side. Kids, dogs, and family sell. Bring a dog, a child, or your family in your video. You will hit a homerun with connecting to your audience.

I have a YouTube channel, and it all started on a crazy idea I had for creating a drink. I had my daughter film a video on her iPhone on how to make a drink called the Chicago Splash. I posted it to YouTube, and from that, my YouTube channel was created.

Check out my videos by searching for "Sue Kouchis." I post many videos about food, exercise, and why the company I work for is the best. Some of my videos are raw and real, but they tell a great story of who I am as a person. Being perfect is impossible—just have fun and be real.

In my years of selling, I never thought I would have my own video studio in my kitchen. If you do plan on posting videos, make sure you get a ring light. It's an amazing tool that will make you look great. Check out this ring light on Amazon. This ring light makes your skin glow.

The title is: "RGBW Clip LED Ring Light 6" 360° Full Color 8 Lighting Scenes 3200K–6500K Dimmable Clip on Desk, Monitor, Laptop, Chair and Bed for Video Conference Lighting, Computer Monitor Light or Vlogging Equipment." Brand: selfila.

DRIP MARKETING STRATEGY

It is a marketing strategy that sends prewritten marketing over a period of time. This is another way of staying in front of your prospect or customer and win customers for life. Drips are used on websites, social media, and email.

This was a game changer for me in the new world of sales. I just learned about drip marketing and the power of marketing. I have a new strategy called the DoubleDrip marketing concept. Our company sends out drip marketing to prospects and customers, and I follow up with a personal drip. What I mean by personal drip, is that I send out personal videos, marketing material or market intelligence, connecting the prospect or customer with a solution to their needs. Be careful not to annoy your customer or prospect with the automated drips. In my own experience, I tend to delete the automated. Remember, in this world of sales, you need sixteen touches before a customer will respond.

Have fun and be creative with the drip strategy.

Zoom, Zoom, Zoom

For most of us, Zoom is the best way to host virtual meetings. Did you know there is a setting on Zoom to make your skin look ten years younger? You might not need this tip, but it's always good to know that if you're having a bad skin day there's something to help.

Tap or click on the "Settings" menu on your Zoom client. Select the "Video Settings," and then click on the "Touch Up My Appearance" button. This feature irons out any obvious blemishes or marks and helps add an extra layer of polish to your appearance. This is also a great option if you're in a rush and don't have the time to apply any makeup.

CHAPTER FOUR: STRATEGIES AND TIPS

In my years as a sales manager and in field sales, I've found two things are very important: being honest and keeping it simple. You will have a customer for life if you stay true and honest.

Do these seven steps, and you will be on your way to great success:

1. Identify pain points and find their wounds: What's going well and what could be better? It's great to have your customer articulate in their words what they enjoy about their current partnership or vendor, even if it is not yet you. That way, you understand what they value (pleasure). You then want to understand from their perspective *what could be even better?* This question creates a subconscious gap between where the client is and where they would like to be at the next level. If you can create enough pain of them not being at that level yet and make it evident that you are the solution, you will be more likely to close a deal.

2. Ask great questions: Questions are the answers. Any sales professional knows the key to a great relationship is do majority of the listening. Rule of thumb is 80 percent listening, 20 percent talking.

3. Give an amazing solution with passion. Add more value than the competition: If you're not fired up about your product or solution, why would your client be? It is imperative you believe in your product. Sales is a transference of emotion. Motion is created by emotion.

4. Ask your customer for the next steps: If you ask the customer for the next step, followed by a strong pause and silence, they will respond. Asking for next steps will put you in a place of certainty—it might not be pleasant—if they say the deal is dead, but you can pivot and come up with another strategy. Or the customer might give you the green light and add more opportunities to the mix! Keep changing your approach to success. Never be afraid to ask for the next step! It's important your client articulates in their own words the benefit of working with you, why it is a must, etc. Because if *you* say it, they can argue or negotiate. If they say it, it's true.

5. Ask for leads: Majority of sales professionals don't ask for referrals or leads. I prefer the word *leads* because people are saturated with the word *referral*, and it can feel like too much work for the client. A lead is simply someone they know who can use your service. And ask them, "John, which do you think is better: A warm lead or a cold lead?" In a playful way, then politely request they tap the lead and warm them up. You can build your entire business off referrals and leads if you simply work it!

6. Ask for the business: Sounds simple, but you'd be surprised how many people never ask the question. Don't be afraid of making money!

7. Never give up: Resiliency, hunger, and drive make a professional in this environment. Declare it to yourself that you're the type of person who will *go until* you've gotten to your destination.

This formula is my secret sauce to *success*. Many salespeople never ask for leads (I forget sometimes), or never ask for the business or never follow up after the first ghost or rejection email or phone call. That's why moving the body, drinking water, and having positive energy are vital to never ever giving up.

But remember: with many nos, there is a yes just around the corner. Another great tip is to know who the top producer in your company or field is and find out their strengths. How did they get to the top? What are some of their strategies? Once you identify their strategies, they will give you a greater head start with your sales strategy approach. With your newfound energy, the six hot tips mentioned above, and knowing the strength of the top producer of your company or field, you'll be on the road to great success.

Many people fail because they're not true believers in what they're selling. If you genuinely believe with passion that you have the best service or product, success will come. I recently sent a personal video to Warren Buffett at @BerkshireHathaway. I had absolute confidence my company could help Berkshire Hathaway with their supply chain global needs. Why not start at the top of the company? In case you're wondering, no response from Warren yet!

In chapter 3, I mentioned my husband made a power pivot in his business. My husband's business is signage. His main pillar is sign application for many retail stores. So, when the pandemic hit and most retail stores were shut down on Michigan Avenue, his business came to a screeching halt.

Pete, my husband, had many emotions that came over him. But he said it was the time to show his gratitude. He delivered over a hundred free restaurant signs to local businesses that said, "We are open for takeout." In the meantime, he made a stand with plexiglass that could easily be moved in bar areas to create more seating space at the bar.

He always told me that he was not a salesperson. Well, with his passion and the value he was giving to his customers, he sold many of these stands just on cold calls alone. Pete had absolute certainty and confidence that his product would create value and would bring more ROI to the bottom line for the struggling restaurants.

That is the very definition of a power pivot shift, and I am so proud of his drive for gratitude and passion.

INVEST IN YOURSELF

Too often we don't take time to invest in our health, our relationships, and our finances. Read books and attend seminars. This is a great way to learn, and you should always challenge yourself to learn new things. In the last three years, I have made a strong commitment in investing in myself. I deserve it. For years I had the fear of not wanting to spend the money on investing in my personal growth. Deep down, I was in a comfort zone and made excuses for not wanting to grow. I believe there are many people reading this book who have the same belief. I have learned so much about personal growth, health, and the power of gratitude. I now have an Energy wall of success—sticky-note quotes from amazing speakers I have invested in—and I'm so happy I did. This is a daily reminder of positive energy. I have a few of my own quotes I added to the positive wall.

Take up something you've always wanted to learn. I started playing guitar at fifty-eight years old, with not one ounce of musical knowledge. Through YouTube learning, I now have two original songs. Go figure! My husband says I sound great after two bottles of wine.

If we're not growing, we are dying.

I talk about moving the body for energy. Keep exercising and being physically fit. Energy is the key to great sales success. I still play tennis every week to keep fit.

CHAPTER FIVE: TOOLS AND PLATFORMS FOR SUCCESS

Linked In is one of the most powerful tools we currently have to connect with potential customers. I highly recommend building your connections on LinkedIn with CEOs, presidents, CFOs, and vice presidents at companies that you're targeting as prospects. Use LinkedIn as a prospect source rather than a job source.

Did you know that through LinkedIn you can send video and audio messages? These are total game changers. I've used them in my sales process and I've had huge success throughout the pandemic. Prospects want to see and hear who they're dealing with. This could be extremely uncomfortable to some people, so practice on your family member or friends. And remember: repetition is one of the keys to success. When you are reaching out to prospects, send them a voice text through the LinkedIn. Make it short and sweet and get to the point, don't worry about being perfect.

To send an audio message, open the LinkedIn app on your phone. Tap on "Messaging" in the bottom bar. Open the conversation with the person you want to send the voice message to. Tap the microphone icon on the keyboard to bring up the voice-messaging menu. Tap and hold the blue circular microphone button to record your voice message, and then release to send the message.

To send a video to someone on LinkedIn, tap the camera icon labeled "Attach an image." You can choose your video from your phone library or computer library. Also, this is a great feature to send information about your products or services. Another great tip is recording a video outside your prospects business. This will show you care and will make you stand out from the competition.

Too many times sales go sideways because we fail to find the correct decision maker at the company. We've all been there. So start your LinkedIn connection from the top. Once you connect with someone from the C-suite, send them a video or audio message. I've used this tool, and it's been massively successful for me. Make your audio or videos short and to the point.

Every morning I "like" my customers' and prospects' posts on LinkedIn and other social media platforms. It doesn't cost anything, takes up very little time, and makes me feel good while spreading kindness. Try to be the first person to like or comment on someone's post—you'll be noticed. It's human nature to want to see who likes their posts.

LinkedIn shares birthdays and anniversaries, too. This is great time to wish your prospects and customers good wishes. These small gestures go a long way to creating a connection with your prospect or customer! This tip is so simple, and it's free. Every morning I am up early, liking posts and sending good wishes. It's a great start to my day and makes me feel awesome.

Helping your prospect or customer with job applications is another very good tip. The payoff could be large if you place a good candidate at the company. This has been a game changer in my career. I recently helped an old customer get placed in one of my new targets. With her knowledge of our company and great service, we were selected as a logistics provider. Connecting people is a good way to build relationships with customers and prospects.

I have connected love matches as well. Funny story: Back in the day, in the early 1990s, I was working for a small messenger and airfreight company. This company was big on Chicago Cubs outings and lunches. So I decided to bring a few customers to the Cubs game on a blistering hot sunny afternoon. Anyone who has been to Wrigley Field—the baseball stadium and home to the Chicago Cubs—knows how hot the bleachers can get at noon.

John and Kelly were my customers, and they were both single (names changed to protect their identities). John went to the restroom in the third inning, and I asked Kelly if she thought John was cute. She replied that he was not her type. I said "OK, no issues." In my mind, I thought maybe they might be a good match.

Well, I'm not sure what happened, but things turned around. When I left in the fifth inning and came back an hour later, Kelly and John were sitting together very cozy. Turns out Kelly and John started dating and eventually got married.

This was great for business! I got two great accounts from this love match.

ZOOMINFO.COM SALES TOOL

Another useful tool is ZoomInfo.com. It's a platform that helps with discovering new prospective customers, and gives information on top executives, like email and cell phone numbers. This platform gives the latest scoops on companies and is a great resource to help understand the needs of your customer. It also gives three competitors names for the company you're researching. The blue export tab below is linked to Salesforce. You can add your prospects information right into sales force.

Check out the Home Depot page on Zoominfo.com. You see the executives on the right side and the competition on the left side of the page.

During the pandemic, I used the information I got from ZoomInfo, and made my first contact with the CEOs or C-suite people. I sent personal videos and followed up with a call on their cell phone. To date, not one CEO has hung up on me. I always, ask, "Is this a good time to chat? Did you receive my video?" About 60 percent of all my new business starts with the C-suite. I call it the "top-down strategy." Don't be afraid to make your first contact with the CEO or President of the company. Take a drink of water, move your body, smile, and call! They're waiting for you.

In the new world of sales, be consistent with your approach. Also, don't be afraid to change your approach or strategy. If it's not working, never give up; there is always another way to win your customer forever. Make sure you know who your ideal customer is. By this I mean, your customer for forever.

ZoomInfo's CEO, Henry Schuck, gave me ZoomInfo's top five sales plays. Check it out:

ZoomInfo's BDR Team's Top 5 Sales Plays

Sales plays are foundational to go-to-market success.

Here's how ZoomInfo's Chief Operating Officer, Chris Hays puts it: "One of the things I've learned into in my career is that for a sales team to prosper and grow, you have to analyze what works, then rinse and repeat. We call this rinse and repeat process 'sales plays', and they've been the cornerstone of our go-to-market success. Great sales plays are where the art and science of going to market converge."

ZoomInfo's BDR team is about 200+ people strong, and they've been the tip of the spear for ZoomInfo's growth from startup to public company with $500MM in sales in 2020.

Brian Vital, ZoomInfo's VP of Business Development, has orchestrated the many "sales plays" his team has used through the years.

Here, he shares five sales plays that have been wildly successful for ZoomInfo. Many of them can be fully automated through our Workflows product.

For each sales play, we briefly describe:

- ✓ The triggering event
- ✓ Filtering we use
- ✓ The action we take
- ✓ The messaging we use
- ✓ Brian shares thoughts on why he thinks these particular plays work with

zoominfo

SALES PLAY #1:

Funding event

THE TRIGGER
Using ZoomInfo's Funding Intelligence, we implement a trigger when a company has a funding event (e.g. a company receives $10 in a Series A funding round).

FILTERING WE USE
Company that fits our ideal customer profile (ICP) criteria (i.e., is a B2B company; is in certain industries; is based in the US, Australia, or England).

THE ACTION
We pass the contact records through for all people with sales and sales ops roles that are VP and above to Salesforce and our sales engagement tool to begin an email and calling campaign.

THE MESSAGING
Our GTM Intelligence can help you fuel your growth.

BRIAN'S THOUGHTS ON WHY THIS PLAY WORKS

We know that funding means growth is top of mind for these accounts. ZoomInfo can certainly help them accomplish their growth goals with data for go-to market plans. If we manage to get a conversation with a decision maker right after they get funding, I like our odds."

zoominfo

SALES PLAY #2:

Spiking Intent

THE TRIGGER

Using ZoomInfo's Funding Intelligence, we implement a trigger when a company has a funding event (e.g. a company receives $10 in a Series A funding round).

FILTERING WE USE

Company that fits our ideal customer profile (ICP) criteria.

THE ACTION

We pass the contact records through for all people with sales, sales/marketing ops, and marketing roles that are VP and above to Salesforce and our sales engagement tool to begin a targeted email and calling campaign.

THE MESSAGING

The best B2B companies are focused on how to use go-to-market as part of their marketing and sales strategy.

BRIAN'S THOUGHTS ON WHY THIS PLAY WORKS

"This works exceptionally well because we are targeting accounts that are further in the buying cycle than just cold-outreach. We typically see a faster sales cycle for the demos booked from spiking intent signals."

Z zoominfo

SALES PLAY #3:

Competitor technology

THE TRIGGER

When we detect a company uses a competitor technology (e.g. Dun & Bradstreet).

FILTERING WE USE

N/A (company has shown a willingness to pay for GTM data).

THE ACTION

We target contacts with sales and marketing operations titles, and we add them into Salesforce and our sales engagement tool to begin a targeted email and calling campaign.

THE MESSAGING

You save money, reduce complexity, and improve adoption when you consolidate your sales and marketing tech stack.

BRIAN'S THOUGHTS ON WHY THIS PLAY WORKS

"I think most sellers agree that it's easier to replace a spend than create a new spend. In this case, the company already knows the value of data; it's now on us to convey that ZoomInfo is the best solution—which we are, so it's relatively easy."

Z zoominfo

SALES PLAY #4:

Website visits

THE TRIGGER

Using ZoomInfo WebSights, we detect website traffic from a specific company to "down funnel" pages on ZoomInfo's website (e.g. pricing or product pages).

FILTERING WE USE

Company that fits our ideal customer profile (ICP) criteria.

THE ACTION

We notify the BDR via email to evaluate the company based on firmographic and technographic insights we have about the company.

THE MESSAGING

Messaging is dependent on what pages on the ZoomInfo website we see the company is spending time on and customize our messaging and qualifying questions accordingly.

BRIAN'S THOUGHTS ON WHY THIS PLAY WORKS

"Inbound demos without inbound form-fills? That's the beauty of this, prospects are on your website and are in the market. Pass these contacts to your outbound folks and have them go after these 'window shopping' accounts."

Z zoominfo

IDEAL CUSTOMER

Let's face it: some customers suck the life out of us. You need to know who your ideal customer is and work on mastering the power of bringing value—more value than your competition, servicing at the highest level. Don't be afraid to "fire" a customer if they truly are not coming from a place of true partnership.

If they mistake your kindness for weakness, it's time to end the partnership. This is hard for me as a sales professional. I always want to make everyone happy. I believe the door is always open, but sometimes you need know when to close the door and lock it. In your heart, you know when the time is right. But in the world of sales, you can always find the key to reopen the door and start fresh.

Nos, Ghosting, and Crickets

You know what I'm talking about! When you don't hear back from your prospect, it can drain your drive and energy. This can happen at any point during the sales process, and unfortunately many salespeople give up on the sale too soon.

Let me share a quick story: The president of our company sent me a sales lead of a customer that ships medical equipment from Germany to the US. Now, when the president of your company gives you a lead, you attack it as quick as possible and hope for great success. Well, unfortunately, crickets and ghosting were killing my success at this company. I threw all my strategy at this lead and nothing was working. I did, however, uncover a few pain points along the way that were very beneficial. So I said to myself, "Let's change strategy and start at the top." The president of this company was based in Germany, and I used LinkedIn to connect with him. It took a few days and the president accepted my invitation. I sent the president a short personal video introducing myself and offering an amazing solution to one of the pain points I uncovered. After a few more touches and drips he asked that I meet the local US team to explain our solution to their supply chain issues. It turns out I was at the right place at the right time. He told me, "Sue, we needed someone to provide consistent, reliable service, and your personal video gave me confidence that your company was the right choice." After many meetings, I can say this company is one of our top German customers! It all started with crickets and ghosting—go figure!

The professional salesperson who has energy, pivots, and changes strategy will *win*. Did you know, with the new world of selling, sixteen touches or more are needed to get a reaction from a potential customer? Don't give up on the chase, my friends. Your success is right around the corner.

NEVER GIVE UP

Three words for success: *never give up*! Through marketing, video, social media, sales platforms, and cold-calling, your yes is right around the corner. Keep making those small touches for success.

Check out these great stories from successful people who received many nos before the yes. Truly inspiring stories.

IT COSMETICS

Jamie Kern Lima, the founder of IT Cosmetics, sold her brand to L'Oréal for $1.2 billion and became the first female CEO of L'Oréal. She received many nos in her career before she made her true success. Jamie started her dream from her bedroom, not earning income for years and hearing nos from retailers and investors. Her desire, passion, and energy led her nos into a yes. Check out her book *Believe It (How to Go From Underestimated to Unstoppable)*.

KENTUCKY FRIED CHICKEN

Colonel Harland Sanders started traveling by car to different restaurants and cooked his fried chicken on the spot for restaurant owners. If the owner liked the chicken, they would enter into a handshake agreement to sell his chicken. He was turned down 1,009 times before his chicken was accepted once!

By 1964, Colonel Harland Sanders had six hundred franchises selling his trademark chicken. He sold his company for $2 million but remained as a spokesperson. In 1976, the Colonel was ranked as the world's second most recognizable celebrity. It's amazing how the man started at the age of sixty-five, when people most retire, and built a global empire out of fried chicken. It's never too late to build your dream.

Spanx

Sara Blakely, founder of Spanx, was a salesperson, selling fax machines door to door when she came up with the idea for Spanx. The idea came from cutting the feet off her pantyhose and wearing them out. She had many nos before her big break.

"When I graduated from college, I went straight into selling fax machines. I was door-to-door for seven years. Then I cut the feet out of my pantyhose and I've been off promoting Spanx ever since.

"Now, women have been cutting the feet out of their pantyhose for a variety of reasons for twenty years, but no one took the idea and ran with it. I think the difference was the amount of mental preparation I had been doing prior to that day. A lot of thinking, a lot of visualizing, and a lot of goal setting. I was very clear in asking the universe to show me an opportunity and give me my own idea. I had assessed my strengths and weaknesses as a sales rep. I knew I could sell, and I knew I liked people, and I was selling a product I didn't understand or even particularly like. If I could create my own product, one that I actually really liked, I felt I could do better.

"The very first time I cut the feet out of my pantyhose, I knew that was my opportunity. This was what I had been manifesting and thinking about. I thought, 'Thanks! Got it. Gonna run with it.'

"I think that one of the biggest reasons that Spanx exists is that I didn't tell anyone my idea early on. I kept it to myself for one year and pursued it at night and on the weekends. All anybody knew was that Sara was working on some crazy idea. No one told me to do that, it was a completely intuitive feeling. After a year of this, I sat my friends and family down and said, 'It's footless pantyhose.'

"They looked horrified. 'That's what you've been working on?!' It wasn't malicious; there was a lot of love and concern. 'Sweetie, if it's such a good idea, why doesn't it already exist? And even if it is a good idea, those big guys are going to blow you out of the water in the first couple of months.' If I'd heard those things on the day I first cut the feet out of my pantyhose, I think I'd probably still be selling fax machines today.

"I could tell customers why they needed my product in thirty seconds. 'I've invented footless pantyhose so you can wear white pants with no panty lines, look thinner, and wear any style shoe. You've got clothes that have been hanging in your closet for years because you can't figure out what to wear under them. You need this.'

"Then I realized that I could add another layer of impact by making this visual. So I took pictures of my own rear end, me in white pants with Spanx, and me in white pants without Spanx. I brought them to Kinko's and laminated them, and I would stand at the entrance of stores to hook people in.

"If after thirty seconds of explaining 'why you need this product' I still didn't get them, I held up my laminated pictures and they would say, 'Oh, I see … I'll take two!' Talk about putting your butt on the line!"

Sara went door to door selling her Spanx and getting nos and rejection, but eventually her passion and energy led her to a yes with the buyer of the Neiman Marcus Group. Sara tells the story that she changed into the product in the ladies' restroom in the presence of the Neiman Marcus buyer to prove the benefits of her product. The rest is history. Sara is a self-made billionaire and her passion, energy, and vision led her to success.

SYLVESTER STALLONE

Check out this information from the author of *The Strive Team*.

"Most people don't know this about Sylvester Stallone, but he had a dream as a young man to become a big movie star in Hollywood. He longed to become a great director, producer, and writer. But of course, everyone told him it could not be done. But he wasn't one to take no for an answer. And after finding little luck in the New York's films scene, he decided to try his chances in Los Angeles.

"As luck would have it, his life in Los Angeles was not all sunshine and rainbows. He struggled and strived for a few years in Los Angeles as well. At one point, things got so bad and he was so short on money that he had to take his wife's jewelry and sell it without her permission just to make a few extra dollars. He even went through a short period of homelessness, spending a few nights sleeping on the floor of a bus station. But the worst of his dire straits would be when he had to sell his dog because he could barely keep him fed.

"Struggle was a way of life for Sylvester Stallone for many years. But he was willing to suffer through barely making ends meet, so long as he could keep taking shots at roles, regardless of the size. He was willing to go through hell so long as there was the potential to fulfill his dream of making it in Hollywood.

"Fortunately, his trials and tribulations would not last forever. One day after witnessing a boxing match between a virtually no-name boxer—his name was actually Chuck Wepner—who went head-to-head with the greatest of all time, Muhammad Ali, a brilliant idea came to him.

"It is said that after he watched this man take on the champ Ali, even knocking him down at one point, and almost going the entire distance of the fight with him, he became inspired by what he felt was a metaphor for life. In fact, he became so inspired by what he saw, that when he got back home from the fight, he locked himself up in his eight by nine-foot apartment for over three days straight. And when he finally came out of his apartment, he had completed the script that would eventually come to be known as *Rocky*.

"But just having that script in hand didn't mean he was fated to overnight success. No, there were still more obstacles that had to be overcome. The script was written, but Sylvester didn't yet have a backer, a producer for it.

"However, his big opportunity would crystalize after wrapping up a casting call for a film he was auditioning for, a film that was being directed and produced by two notable filmmakers, Robert Chartoff and Irwin Winkler. He didn't make the cut during that audition, but before leaving the set that night he seized his moment while having conversation with Robert Chartoff and Irwin Winkler.

"It was during that conversation that he boldly mentioned his interests in writing along with some of his ideas to the film producers. As fate would have it, they became intrigued enough in what he was saying that they invited him to stop by their office at a later time so they could learn more about him and his ideas. And, as they say, the rest is history.

"Sylvester Stallone's script won over the two filmmakers, and they decided they would buy the script from him so they could make it into a movie. They offered Sylvester Stallone upwards of $300,000, which was the most money he had ever been offered, let alone seen at that time. But he knew that if his script would become a success, he would forever regret not going for the lead role. So he made it a point to star in his own film, [and] after much negotiating, he would eventually decline upwards of $360,000 for the sale of his script alone. He eventually won out in his negotiations and sold his script for $25,000, but on the condition that he would get to star in the lead role.

"Sylvester Stallone's calculated risk to forgo what was a huge pay out at the time for his script, has made all the difference in his ultimate success. The *Rocky* movie has since gone on to become a smash hit, along with a series of related cascading blockbuster successes—successes that Sylvester Stallone proclaims he could have never imagined in wildest dreams.

"And it all happened because he had a success ethos of never settling. It happened because he was willing to embrace the pain and suffering of being without, until his vision was realized. He was willing to take on the hits of life, and willing to lose it all to strike it big. And it is because he had a vision of what he wanted, and stuck to it till the end, that he realized his vision, got everything he wanted, and struck it big. Sylvester Stallone's now has one of the most sizeable net worths in Hollywood, and he is arguably one of the most successful and well-known actors of all time."

I want to share my own story of Never Give UP! I was calling on this company for 5 years and every time I would drop in, the VP of Operations, Purchasing Mgr and Logistics Mgr would say, "all is great" with their present supplier. They were using the same company for 11 years. My goal at this company was not to talk about price but show them my energy and passion for my company. They never kicked me out, I would admire their strong partnership they built with their supplier. I did have one crazy strategy, my husband who is in the sign and graphics business, armed me with oversized business cards, pre covid, I used these oversize business cards on long-shots, meaning (not enough pain for customers to switch). So, on this account, this customer would line their cubicles with these oversize business cards, every time I would drop in, it was a big joke. They said Sue, if we ever need your service, we have your number and email at our fingertips.

With Covid, everything was shut down and I could not make the small touches and deliver in person my oversized business cards. That didn't stop me! I sent my personal video's and kept in touch by LinkedIn marketing and drips. On a Thursday, I was sent a personal email on Linkedin from the VP of Operations, he wrote, Sue, please call me, we might have an opportunity. When I called him right back, he wanted me to have our RIM team come in on the following Monday to discuss implementation and a start date. They had a big falling out with their supplier of 11 years. And the first person they thought of was the RIM team. The VP told me, my strong passion for my company was convincing to take a chance on RIM to help them with their urgent supply chain needs. We did meet in person, that was our first team RIM sales call in a year in half. The morale of this story is, no hard selling was needed, my energy and passion brought home this great victory. I have also learned that if you come from a place of PASSION, ENERGY and SINCERITY, no company you're calling on is a waste of TIME. Some people will probably disagree, but I have firsthand proof, that being patient and bringing the Positive Energy will win in the end.

As the old saying goes "Never Give Up".

CHAPTER SIX: KEEP IT REAL

The secret to life success is gratitude.

The definition of gratitude is the "quality of being thankful; readiness to show appreciation for and to return kindness."

This is another game changer for me. The amount of joy I feel when I'm giving my time, talent, and treasures is indescribable. I feel so good. Practice gratitude every day and you will see the energy and passion in fulfilling a successful life.

Getting involved with your local community, food bank, shelters, charities, your church, or giving back in any way is a great way to feel the positive energy. Money is not the key driver to happiness and success. Money will always come to you when you come from a place of gratitude. Keep it real and have a healthy mind, body, and soul. Giving back your time, talent, and treasures to help a cause you're passionate about will bring you great joy. I recently participated in a Feed6 charity organization at our church. We packed fifty thousand meals for the homeless. This was a great community builder and a small way to give back our time.

Think about the last time you did something special for someone, whether it was small or large. A simple smile or wave to someone you don't know goes a long way. Give a free cup of coffee to a stranger at a coffee shop, buy someone's gas at the pump, buy a stranger a breakfast, lunch, or dinner. Work at a food shelter or something that excites you! Something good will happen to you. This is the power of giving back.

They say the top 1 percent of professionals give back most of their income to change the world.

Everyday gratitude list (wave, smile, or spreading time, talent, and treasures)

1.
2.
3.
4.
5.

Keep it simple—don't complicate life!

Chapter Seven: Happy Family, Happy Life

Yes, a happy family is essential to sales success.

Not many sales seminars or sales books talk about having a happy family and a happy life for true success. How many people have you known in your lifetime who have all the money in the world and are successful, but they're downright miserable? I can think of many.

The curveballs of life will always hit us when we least expect it. The true secret is having positive energy. Get the family moving toward positive energy. Great energy starts with eating healthy and moving the body. Keep working on this path to success.

Our family always ate dinner together on Sundays, and we discussed the highs and lows of the day. This was a great conversation starter. Getting the whole family to connect with sharing wins and challenges of the day will keep communication flowing. Date night for couples is also important to a happy life. Bike rides, jumping out of plane, dinners, or taking a walk together will bring lasting joy and happiness. My husband, Pete, and I have been together for thirty-one years, and date night is always on the calendar. And *yes*, one of our date nights was jumping out of a plane.

Wow, that was an *energy* crank.

Staying connected with family is the ultimate driver for life success.

This quote from Warren Buffet sums it up.

CHAPTER EIGHT: CREATE YOUR OWN STORY FOR SUCCESS

L ife will never be the same. Now is the time for "Pivot Power" and to be creative with your own story of success.

Now is the time to create your own success. Do not wait; take massive action.

Now is the time to crush your fears that robbed you from success.

Now is the time to start moving your body for success.

Now is the time to invest in yourself and create a positive journey.

Now is the time to get healthy with going to the dentist and booking those yearly health checkups. Now is the time to embrace the nos and work toward the yes that is right around the corner.

Now is the time to start loving your partner to achieve your "peak state."

Now is the time to keep changing your approach to sales success.

Now is the time! Take massive action for success. You got this. Life is just beginning.

Now is the time to take those curveballs life throws at you and crush them with your own positive story.

If you come from a world of gratitude and love, nothing can stop you.

Are we ready?

Hell yes, I am ready. Let's go!

I'm so excited for your journey!

EPILOGUE

I was inspired to write this book because of my family and my mother, Sweet Georgia. My mom was always my number-one sales manager. She always told me, "Sue, no matter what curveball is thrown at you, positive energy will always win in the end."

One hundred percent of profits from this book will go to the Outreach Program and their local affiliate, Feed6.

The mission of the Outreach Program is to provide safe water, food, medical care, and education to children and those in need at home and abroad: https://outreachprogram.org.

Feed6 currently organizes meal-packaging events in Illinois, Wisconsin, Indiana, and Michigan. Volunteers come together to package nutritional meals of macaroni and cheese fortified with soy and vitamins—many multiples more nutritious than popular brands available in the supermarket. Each plastic package our volunteers lovingly create can feed six children. www.feed6.org.

Chris Coyne, Co-Founder
The Feed6 Movement
www.Feed6.org
EMAIL: ccoyne@Feed6.org
CELL: 954.478.5400

Learn about Feed6: www.Feed6.org
Check out our video collection at: ww.feed6.org/event-videos.html
Learn about Outreach: www.outreachprogram.org
Watch the Outreach Story: http://www.feed6.org/media.html

Keep smiling! The best is yet to come!

Sweet Sue and Sweet Georgia (Sue's mom)

With love,
Sweet Sue